I write this with all sincerity  my previous books I know th, gratitude is a beautiful thing to share.

Thank you for trusting me to share these messages and be the voice that encourages you to shift your energy. Spiritual journey's are different for everyone and that can make them seem overly complicated because there is *so* much to learn about.

I strongly encourage you to find what resonates with your soul. My suggestions may not align with what feels 'right' with your soul and that is perfectly normal! Follow your intuition and do what resonates with you.

Energy is a powerful tool and if you trust yourself you'll begin to see just how incredible your own intuition truly is.

There is no wrong way when it comes to your energy. It's *your* energy. It's *your* space. Do what feels right and learn along the way. Have fun with your experience and be patient with yourself. It might be frustrating at first, but I promise that it's worth the journey.

Do what sets your soul on fire...

Table of Contents

The Basics (1)

Associations (5)

The Name (8)

Simmer Pot Recipes (9)

Sun Water (19)

Activities (21)

A Deeper Look (23)

Oranges and Lemons (24)

Maypole & Mini Maypole (25)

Animal Symbolism (31)

Fairy vs Faerie (32)

Fire Without The Flame (33)

Journal Prompts (35)

Final Word (68)

Beltane
The Basics

As we come out of a place of balance (spring equinox) we begin to enter the phase of sun energy. Beltane is celebrated on May 1st in the northern hemisphere. It is a time when the veil is thin – something you probably hear around Samhain. Samhain (October 31 – November 1) can be viewed as a time of preparing for winter, rest, reflection, and relaxation. Beltane is the opposite of that. It is celebrated with fire, light, the sun, and is a time for action.

During Beltane and the coming weeks we honor fertility, sex, unions, abundance, and growth. We are (or rather, should be) coming out of a time of reflection and finding balance. It is now time to take what we've learned and make the changes we've been planning.

I find a good way to look at Beltane is movement. The winter solstice was a time to rest. Imbolc (generally celebrated February 1 – 2) is a time to begin to wake up & stretch. The spring equinox is a time to find our footing (balance). Beltane is a time to put one foot in front of the other and move forward.

Beltane is often celebrated with fire and light. As much as we would all love to attend a massive bon fire in the forest with a large group of friends and family as we dance and feast, it's probably just not realistic. Your celebrations to honor this period do not need to be extravagant. Have a bonfire with friends, use battery operated candles to create an ambiance indoors if you can't have an open flame, or set your intentions and make sun tea.

I strongly encourage you to adjust if you see something in this book that you love but know it's just not feasible with where you are in life right now. If you aren't in a position to have a bonfire, then make a plan to get up early and watch the sunrise. There are always options. Find ways to honor Beltane that work for where you are in life right now and within your budget. Please do not get discouraged if the way you celebrate looks differently than someone else's. We are all on our own journey and we aren't here to compare our lives with each other.

Action • Movement • Growth • Passion

I know I spent time emphasizing that Beltane is very much about passion and fiery energy, but there is also a softer side to Beltane. After all, we are still in spring.

Floral crowns, ribbons, and faeries are very strong associations with this time of the year. We are transitioning out of the pastel colors from the spring equinox into more vibrant colors - and more confident decisions.

The important word there was transition. There is a gentleness that can be found within the bold transition of rebirth as we enter Beltane. We don't just jump from night into day. We have dawn before the sunrise and we have dusk just after sunset before the nightfall.

Let your soul bloom.

Beltane
Associations
Herbs, Flowers & Foods

rosemary
mint
lemonade
bread
honey
daffodils
dandelions
tulips
fresh salad
egg
ivy
rose
violet
mugwort

blessed thistle
marjoram
nettle
primrose
rose
lily of the valley
coriander
snapdragon
vanilla
peach
frankincense
jasmine
dill
coltsfoot
lilac

daisy
strawberry
cakes
cherries
dairy
red wine
oatmeal
marigold
sandalwood
lemon
asparagus
lemon balm
ginger
spearmint
moss

It is important to research each ingredient before use, especially if you have pets. Certain flowers can be toxic.

Beltane
Associations

Colors
green, yellow, blue, pink, white, lavender, magenta, vivid blue, red

Animals
dove, bee, goat, frog, rabbit, butterfly, horse, alpaca, bluebird, cat, swan, leopard, swallow

Crystals
aventurine, emerald, jade, malachite, rose quartz, tourmaline, rhodonite

Mythical Creatures
faeries, unicorn, satyr

Spiritual Beings
green man, oak king, pan, herne, gaia, flora, maeve, bel

Beltane Intentions

fertility	passion
abundance	love
confidence	self improvement
action	cleansing
creativity	protection
prosperity	gratitude
beauty	growth
youth	union
connections	psychic awareness

Beltane Symbols

maypoles, basket of flowers, flower crowns, ribbons, wreaths, phallic symbols, bonfires, baskets, candles, seeds, cauldron, chalice, music

Beltane
The Name

I know I briefly touched on what Beltane is, but I felt it was important to dive a little deeper into it.

Beltane is Gaelic and translates to, 'the fires of Bel' or 'bright fire'. It is assumed that Bel is a reference to the Celtic sun god, Belenus.

Belenus translates to, "the Shining God". There is a recent disagreement if the Celts worshiped Belenus as the sun god, but it could come down to translations over time.

Belenus is associated with the sun, light, healing, and prophecy. He is often called upon for divination work.

On Beltane, a fire is lit to set intentions for fertility & abundance. It was also a time to purify, cleanse, and be re-born. Some also say that the fire would be used to pray for protection as well.

Beltane is generally celebrated on May 1st to mark the halfway point between the spring equinox and summer solstice. It should also be noted that this is also widely celebrated as the start of summer in Ireland.

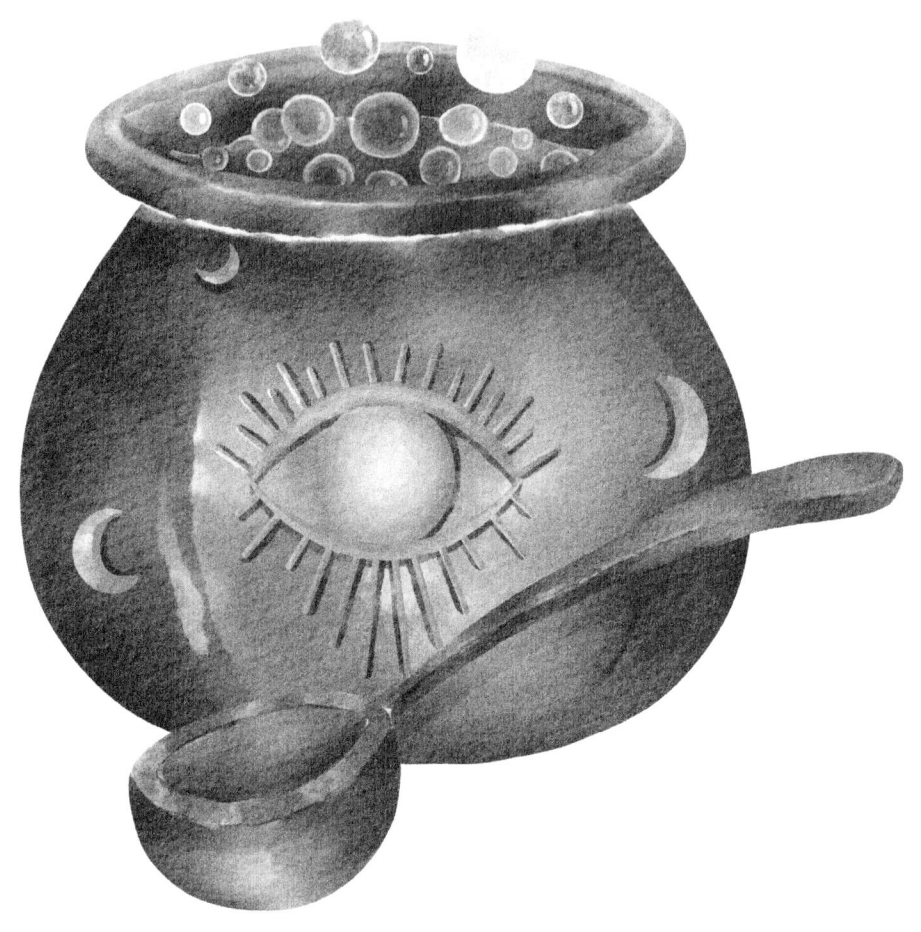

Simmer Pot Recipes
Beltane

 # Before you begin...

You'll notice there are no measurements in any of my recipes. I personally prefer a mini simmer pot - which in most cases is actually just a butter warmer. They're powered by tea light so you aren't leaving your stove on all day or something plugged in for hours. You can absolutely use a stovetop or crockpot if that's your preference.

If you are using something powered by tea light, I find that the aroma comes out best if you 'dip' your ingredients (stirring is difficult in smaller pots) and burn through at least (2) tea light candles. I suggest using these in smaller spaces such as a bedroom.

The aroma is softer, but can definitely fill a space. I am extremely sensitive to strong smells, even essential oil. Simmer pots have allowed me to create a safe and calming space while still getting to enjoy beautiful aromas - without all the chemicals that candles have.

Use as much, or as little, of an ingredient as you feel you need.

Some things I (unfortunately) have to make clear:

- Never leave your lit simmer pot left unattended
- Keep out of reach of children & pets
- I am not responsible for any allergic reactions
- Don't eat or drink the contents
- Wait for your simmer pot to cool before emptying or cleaning it
- Outcomes of using metaphysical products are not guaranteed

Beltane Associations

Simmer Pot Recipe

Coriander
To boost confidence, help heal emotional trauma, and bring in fire energy.

Vanilla
Said to enhance connections, offer protection, and encourage a new way of thinking for ideas.

Ginger
To draw in passion, confidence, and prosperity.

Strawberry
Said to assist with creativity. Attracts favorable circumstances & increase happiness.

Cherry
A sign of rebirth. Said to assist with intuition.

Blessed Thistle
Strength, protection and joy. Said to renew vitality and increase strength.

Fertility
Simmer Pot Recipe

Nettle
binding · healing · courage · protection · banishing

Dandelion
growth · manifestation · happiness · hope · the sun

Jasmine
psychic powers · abundance · fertility · sensuality

Lemon
happiness · rejuvenation · mood booster

Rose
unconditional love · lust · uncrossing

*Fertility can refer to pregnancy, abundance, birth, life, and attracting what we want to grow.

Confidence
Simmer Pot Recipe

Black Pepper
To remove blockages preventing you from seeing your own strength.

Mugwort
To help connect with your Higher Self.

Raspberry
A reminder to be kind to yourself and not get hung up on the past as you grow into the confident version of yourself.

Rosemary
To call back your power and remember who you are.

Peppermint
For clarity to help remove any doubts.

Connections

Simmer Pot Recipe

Rose
To create a calm and loving environment. Said to connect souls who are 'good' for each other.

Lemon
To help connect with your Higher Self.

Thyme
To bring out the good in those around you.

Bay Leaf
Said to smooth over disagreements & carry your troubles away.

Lavender
To encourage harmony between you and those you are spending time with.

What To Do With Simmer Pots Afterwards

"What do I do with the ingredients afterwards?" I hear that question a lot. I honestly never put a lot of thought into this because it was always second nature for me to find ways to get the most out of the ingredients I was using.

If there is salt in your recipe...
Never give your recipe directly back to earth. Salt will dry out & destroy the soil & anything growing there. With that said, you can rinse the salt and continue to the other suggestions.

If there is no salt in your recipe...
One option is to simply give your ingredients back to earth. Dig a small hole & bury the ingredients, put the seeds or berries in a bird feeder, scatter the ingredients around the perimeter of your home, or even release your ingredients down running water such a stream or river.
Use your own discretion if something is toxic to animals or would be better off buried rather than scattered on the surface.

The following ideas can be done with or without salt. *Again, use your own discretion.*

You could make a room spray by straining the solids and putting the liquid into a spray bottle. Add a little witch hazel to stabilize the spray if you're keeping it for more than two or three days.

Use the liquid to rinse your hands. Return the solids back to earth.

Put the solids into a biodegradable (or reusable) tea bag and add it to your intentional bath or shower.

I also understand that all of the above just might not be something you're able to do. We all have different situations and I completely understand that. If you're not able to return your ingredients back to earth just be sure to dispose of your simmer pots mindfully.

What does mindfully actually mean? Basically, be intentional when you throw your ingredients out. Don't just toss them in the trash and call it a day. Show gratitude for their use and having the opportunity to be fortunate enough to use them.

Don't wait to be confident to make moves. Be courageous and the confidence will follow.

Sun Water

Making sun water is going to depend on your intention for the water itself. If you intend on drinking any of the moon water you make, be sure that you're starting with drinking water.

Sun water can be used to add to your simmer pots, to drink, to use in a ritual bath, to water plants with, etc.

If you're going to add crystals to your water please be sure that you research the crystals being used and that they are safe to put in water.

For some like myself, sun water is comforting. There is a warmth about it. For some, the sun energy is too chaotic. There is no right or wrong answer. I personally love using sun water in my simmer pots. Follow what feels right for *you*.

Sun Water

Step 1:
Get a glass container, fill with water, and close with lid.
Step 2:
Set your intentions and place in direct sunlight, if possible. You can leave it on a windowsill or put outside.
Step 3:
Let sit for a few hours or bring inside before the sun goes down.
Step 4:
Store & use as needed. Some people will even cover their jar with a cloth to prevent moonlight from hitting it while in storage. Follow what resonates for you.

The steps above are the simplest form of making sun water. The possibilities are abundant in what you can make with your sun water.

You can even add crystals and herbs to make an infused room spray. Just be sure that with whatever you're doing, you do your research beforehand on the ingredients being used.

Remember, it's your practice.
Follow what resonates for you.

Beltane Activities

- Have a bonfire
- Create a Beltane bowl
- Put on your favorite music and dance
- Plant bulbs
- Sprinkle wildflower seeds that are native to the area
- Create faerie offerings
- Make a mini maypole
- Create (and wear) a flower crown
- Gather wildflowers
- Make lemonade
- Light red, yellow, or orange candles to honor fire
- Spend time outdoors (hopefully with some sunshine!)
- Meditate
- Call a friend who makes you laugh
- Feast with friends and family
- Read your tarot cards
- Show gratitude to the trees
- Decorate your home with flowers
- Read and learn about the fae
- Make a simmer pot
- Decorate with ribbon
- Bring bright, vibrant colors into your home
- Journal

Beltane Activities

- Watch something that makes you laugh & brings joy
- Write down short term goals that you plan on harvesting come the fall
- Make a lemon (or orange) wreath
- Have a picnic
- Add honey to something you eat or drink to make your season sweet
- Take a ritual bath
- Express your love to family & friends
- Set your intentions
- Decorate your alter
- Roast marshmallows
- Dress in red and white
- Bake bread
- Work on self love
- Start a creative project you've been thinking about
- Take action
- Fertility spells (this doesn't need to be for conception)
- Work with your angel team
- Perform a fire ritual
- Honor your body
- Laugh & smile

A Deeper Look

To say that my brain works differently than most is an understatement. I grew up having to be resourceful. It comes naturally to me and I will find a way to make something work.

As I previously mentioned in this book, the possibilities to celebrate Beltane are endless...we just have to get a little creative.

This next part of the book will offer suggestions and alternatives to a few of my favorite ways to celebrate Beltane. I strongly encourage you to let your inner child roam free & have fun with your own celebrations.

Oranges & Lemons

I've found that a lot of associations have changed over the years. A lot of it seems to be that the world has advanced so much, and in such a short period of time, that we now have access to things instantly and can travel easily.

Oranges have a strong association with Yule (the winter solstice) because they represent the sun. I've always found it strange that oranges weren't associated with Beltane.

The two events are honoring the sun in different ways, but the sun & fire are still very much the main focus.

Oranges can represent the sun, success, fire energy, happiness, light, bliss, and attracting prosperity.

Lemons can represent the rays of the sun, purification, joy, rejuvenation, removing blockages, a mood booster, and protection.

While my recipes in this book don't include oranges, you can bet I will be making an orange slice wreath to hang on my door to welcome in prosperity, success, and happiness.

Invite the light into your life in ways that work best for you.

The Maypole

Let's talk about the basics of the maypole. There is evidence that the maypole was originally associated with spring and summer, not necessarily Beltane.

There are a few theories floating around about the symbolism of the maypole, but we don't have any solid proof of the origins. Like most celebrations (or religions) that have been around for centuries, the stories were carried down or translations between languages caused the origins to change.

One theory is that the maypole is a sexual symbol about union. The pole itself representing masculine energy while the flowers and ribbons represent feminine energy. That theory is based on the assumption that the maypole was created for British celebrations to honor the Roman god, Priapus.

Another theory is that the maypole was a way to honor the changing of the seasons. The pole itself being the axis of the earth and the ribbons that are held to dance around representing the changing of the seasons.

I personally think the two theories combined make the most sense. The union of masculine & feminine energy as the seasons change.

The maypole is said to originally have been created using a living tree. Over time, and depending on the culture, the maypole began to vary.

Some locations would cut down a tree to use the trunk as the pole. Others began to use materials they have one hand or that they can dismantle to store and re-use the following year.

Maypoles are also decorated differently around the world. I think at this point in time, most of the decorations depend on what's available and what's realistic. Make do with what you have, right?

The basics are the same. A pole is erected with long ribbons secured at the top. You'll often seen intricate ribbon designs and flowers at the top as well.

They are designed with the intention to dance around them, so the ribbons are long enough to not only reach the ground but to also wrap around the pole. Participants will hold the ribbon as they dance around.

Some dances are choreographed while others are just groups of friends there to enjoy the experience and go where the music leads them.

Mini Maypole

I don't know about you, but I don't have a group to gather around the maypole with. There is a great alternative, though! Create a mini maypole for your alter or desk.

At the end of the day it's all about intentions, right? Here's my version of the mini maypole. Remember, this is only a suggestion. Find what works best for you.

What you'll need:

base (slice of wood)
poll (dowel)
ribbon
scissors
hot glue
pipe cleaner or small wood vine wreath
decorations such as moss & flowers

There are a few different ways to make your mini maypole, so I am not going to do a step by step process. I'm hoping this adds a little extra 'nudge' to encourage you to use your creativity. Connect with your inner child and enjoy the ride!

Mini Maypole

You're going to need to find a way to attach your ribbon to the top of your maypole. This is probably the most important detail - and the focal point of your maypole.

You can do this using a small wreath (or some sort of flat circle), pipe cleaner (or something bendable), or simply glue. I personally love the twig wreath, even if it is a little more complicated to 'hang'.

One way to 'hang' your wreath is to hot glue one end of the ribbon to your dowel. Tie the other end of your ribbon around your wreath and knot or hot glue to attach. I recommend starting with your wreath to attach the ribbon, waiting until all of your strands are attached, and then working on attaching the side that will connect directly to the dowel.

I know someone is reading this and thinking, 'why is she making this so complicated?' The truth is, I didn't want to create a step by step guide for this process because it would discourage people from thinking outside the box. Use your imagination. This is simply intended to be a guide.

Another way that you could attach your ribbon is simply by gluing one end of your ribbon directly on the dowel and letting the other end flow freely. You could also glue that ribbon onto your base (slice of wood) to keep it in place.

Maybe you are more drawn to the Midsummer pole (which is an entirely different pole, but a similar design concept.)

If I simply said to follow the steps it would eliminate a lot of magic of this experience - how boring!

It might be easier to have your dowel secured to your base (slice of wood) or you might find it best to wait until your ribbon is attached at the top before gluing your dowel to the base.

Once you have pole (dowel) attached to the base (slice of wood) it's time to get creative!

Do you want your ribbon to swirl down the pole? Would flowers add a little pizazz to the top of your pole and help cover up where you glued the ribbon? Could moss glued to the base really brighten things up? Have fun with this and embrace the inner child healing that's sure to come along with it.

If your intention is to keep your maypole for years to come, I suggest using artificial flowers and decorations. Dried flowers are also a great option if they are available, but you'll want to make sure to use extra caution when packing your maypole away for the season as it will be more delicate.

If you plan on not keeping your maypole, natural is best. You can even disassemble your maypole at the end of the season and give what you're able back to nature.

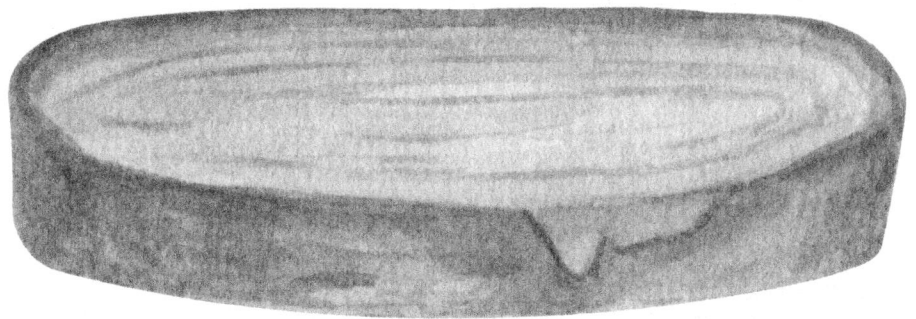

If your plan is to get rid of your maypole at the summer solstice & you are using (untreated) wood as your base, you can add a little extra intention into your work.

Before you assemble your maypole, write your intentions for the season on your wood. You can draw symbols, sigils, words - whatever feels right to you. When you are ready to take your maypole down you can either burn your wood, bury it, or find running water to release it at.

Animal Symbolism

Bumblebee
accomplish the impossible · attract the 'honey' of life · communication · focus

There are many species of bees. For the sake of space, I've chosen the bumble bee to focus on

Goat
creative energy · tranquility · aspiration · confidence · solid footing · abundance · sign of 'good luck' · virility · lust

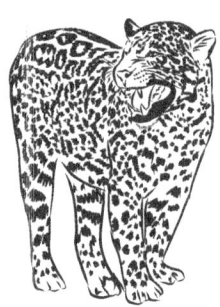

Leopard
strength · courage · power · determination · wisdom · knowledge · future telling · rare beauty · agility

Swallow
divine connection · peace · love · renewal · hope · sign to trust our journey · fertility · loyalty · decisiveness

 # Fairy vs Faerie

This topic has always been fascinating to me. In some areas they are tricksters and in others angel like.

A fairy is said to be kind, helpful, and generous towards humans. A faerie is said to be mischievous, manipulative, and a trouble maker. One legend even says to never give a faerie your full name or it will give them the power to control you.

The story of the fairy has somehow shifted over the centuries and split into two different legends. They originated (as far as I can tell) as messengers from God - sprinkling magic wherever they went. They wanted to offer blessings and help others.

From what I have found, around the 14th century is when the shift started to appear. Britain began spreading folklore that these 'little people' could be evil, and that caused people to start fearing them.

Different mythologies offer different stories & variations in the history with no clear origin.

Pure or mischievous...you decide.

Fire Without The Flame

It seems like whenever I share a simmer pot recipe I read a comment about how someone can't have an open flame. From being in a college dorm to having a bird, there are many different reasons someone may not be able to have an open flame.

So, how do we honor a Beltane without actual fire?

The beauty of living in today's world is that we have a lot of options.

If you are making a simmer pot you could get an inexpensive portable electric stove top. I think I picked one up for around $20 and I am able to use it in other rooms other than the kitchen so it comes in handy!

If you want to create a bowl, or work with any other type of candle magic, use a battery operated candle. I love intentional bowls for this reason: you never have to turn them off or worry about leaving the room. Another great aspect to a bowl is that you use less ingredients. You can use salt as your base (for protection and prosperity) and just a sprinkle of your other ingredients with a battery operated candle in the middle. How simple and effective!

Battery operated candles are also perfect for a display in your home. Clear off the counter or coffee table and set up a little area dedicated to Beltane. You don't need to worry about pets knocking it over or kids accidentally bumping into it.

I talked a bit about lemons and oranges as a symbol for the sun & sun rays. If you don't have battery operated candles or are looking for something different, consider making a 'sun' wreath.

Evenly slice your lemon and/or orange. You'll want to dry them to prevent mold - that can be done either in the oven or a dehydrator. (This is also a great option to save some for future projects or simmer pots!)

Lay out your circle of fruit slices, grab a hot glue gun, and get to gluing each slice. You can also create the bottom later with orange slices for the sun and a smaller circle layered on top of lemons to represent the rays of sunshine. Attach a piece of ribbon or twine on the back and hang where you can enjoy it.

There are always options.

Beltane Journal Prompts

To me, writing is a sacred and very personal experience. Find what feels right for you. You can choose one prompt or all of them. You can write directly in this book or if you're like myself you'll grab a separate notebook and write your responses in that instead. You can draw images for your responses or write out your responses.

Find what works best for you.

What does fire represent to you?

What is your biggest goal today and what are you doing to get you closer to accomplishing that goal?

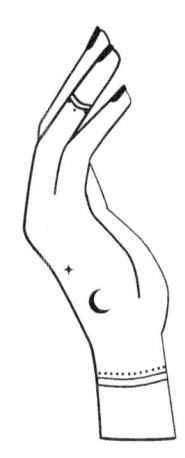

Write about your sexuality.

What are you most passionate about right now?

Write about a romance that sets the world on fire.

Who do you rely on most? Write about them & why the trust is so strong between the two of you.

How often do you laugh? Smile?

Do you thrive more in the summer or winter months?

Think of one person in your life. What light do you bring into their world? What light do they bring into your world?

Are you confident with your sexuality?

Write 5 short terms goals you currently have.

When do you feel most confident?

What is the biggest emotional turn on for you?

What accomplishments do you want to harvest come autumn?

Write about your most passionate romance.

When was the last time you laughed so hard you cried?

What does your perfect alter for Beltane look like?

Think of your favorite fresh flowers. What are they? What do they make you feel? Do you surround yourself with them often or only for special occasions?

What is the biggest emotional turn off for you?

How often do you dance?

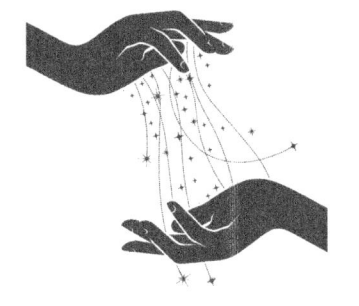

What do doves represent to you?

If you were hosting a gathering tonight, who would you invite? Write why each person you would invite brings light into your life.

Do you find that you hold back when others are around or are you comfortable being yourself with others around? (this includes sharing stories, dancing, crying, etc.)

What brightens your world?

What does celebrating life look like to you?

When was the last time you had an intimate conversation with someone?

What is making you happy right now?

Do you believe that passion and love go hand in hand?

Do you have plants in your living space? Why or why not?

Write one long term goal you are working towards.

Think of a place that rejuvenates your soul. Where is it? Does it hold positive memories?

Write your own Beltane blessing.

A final word...

The information provided in this book is based on my own personal experience and is not to be construed as professional advice. The contents of this book and the resources provided are for informational and entertainment purposes only and do not constitute health, spiritual, or legal advice.

With that said...

Happy Shifting.
xx
jen

Printed in Great Britain
by Amazon